New Survival Projects:

Best DIY Projects for Preppers

Disclaimer: All photos used in this book, including the cover photo were made available under a Attribution–ShareAlike 2.0 Generic (CC BY–SA 2.0)

and sourced from Flickr

Table of Contents

Introduction

Welcome to Homemade Projects for Survival, a D.I.Y. book designed to help you survive some of the most difficult situations in the world and prepare for those situations in a "just in case" environment. With the world in a hammock of chaotic feelings, preparing for the worst has become the norm but most who want to prepare for the worst simply don't know where to start, which is where this book comes into play. From body army, home security, and even portable gardens, this book is designed to cover a wide area of protections and understand how these protections work so the concepts can be applied to other issues. Let's begin.

Chapter 1 – Fortification and Home Security

One of the most important parts about survival is making sure that your enemies take a long time, if not a harder time, to get to you. This includes creating barriers to prevent them from getting in, protecting your body from cutting into your body, and even creating a portable cover as you run away.

Door Barriers

There are a few different methods you can use in order to make sure that coming through that door is one of the most difficult things for them to do. The reason why you want to start with the door is because the door will usually be one of the two common entrances into a home and this means you can block them from getting through this hole into your house. Your house can be made into a fortress with the right modifications, but this will require some work and dedication.

Door Stopper

First, right off the bat, in order to block them from pushing their way into the door you can just put a bar of wood on the bottom of the door and secure it to the ground, but you have to be careful.

You do not want to put a bar of wood that will not be removed in front of any door that you plan to go in and out of. Therefore, the best way to secure the bar of wood is to grab two metal cylinders that will not bend when you sit on them and drill two holes into both the wood and the floor for the metal to fit through. You want to measure as you go, but the goal is to get the metal just above the boards so that you can pull them out without much of a hassle but also ensuring that they are still secured into the ground.

Additionally, this door stopper needs to be as close as possible to the bottom of the door as reasonably possible. The less room the door has to move, the less kinetic energy that the door can produce. Kinetic energy is the scientific terms used to describe the potential force something has when it is moving and the faster something moves, the more kinetic energy that something *will* have. Therefore, the more room you leave something like a door or a window to swing, the more likely that door or window will have more power to break whatever is blocking it.

Securing the Hinges

Another way of protecting the door is to protect the actual hinges. The easiest way to do this is to 3D print a copy for your hinges. However, not all of us have access to a 3D printer therefore we will go over the options you can use if you don't have one.

The first method would be to either use plastic that you melted or you can easily just use hardening caulk glue. Certain types of caulk glue can be hardened to the point where it feels almost impossible to get the nail out of the hinge. However, you do have to be careful here because the caulk will not seal properly and you also have to be careful about whether or not the caulk glue gets in underneath the nail on the hinge. This is because you do not want to have hinge stuck to the nail of the hinge or else the door simply won't open.

If you turn to the right one, you can normally just put the glue over on one side of the hinge, then bring it over the nail and then on to the other side of the hinge. While this is the cheapest method of securing your hinges, just like, really, anything that is cheap it is also the least productive. Normally you won't be able to protect against anyone who has a large amount of experience with unhinging doors. This will generally protect you from the kids trying to get in and provide you with security theater for those of us that simply don't know how to do it.

Melted plastic on the other hand can be quite effective since you can usually wrap the melted plastic around the bottom of the hinges and this will prevent the removal of the plastic but caulk will normally break whenever it's pulled on. The more dense the plastic you can grab, the less likely they will to be able to break it. As an example of this, even though hard hats are made of plastic, the density of the particles inside of the plastic is usually more than that of something like a action figure. As a result, a bowling ball that is dropped on the hard hat will generally bounce off while the same bowling ball dropped on a toy will usually break the toy.

Medieval Gate

Perhaps the easiest method of making sure that a person's ability get past the door without using some sort of massive weapon is difficult is to actually bar the door. While you may find that some other online tutorial tells you that you need a K-bar so that you can hold a door up, the easiest method of barring a door is to just buy two massive hooks, preferably closed, and then a pole to go through them. Place the hooks on either side of the door, as close to the door as possible, and put the pole through them. The metal of the pole makes it difficult to push through in the first place and this pole can be replace with heavier/denser materials that are harder to bend. The closeness to the door prevents the door from having enough kinetic force to push the door open.

Chapter 2 – Getting Energy

Something that many survivalists forgo is talking about a situation that is very difficult to prepare for. These people tend to be in it for the money, but when you need to survive the problem with training to survive in the woods or the desert is simply not the same as doing so in a human environment. If you are in a hostile area or an area effect by a break down in society, one of the key solutions is to get out of the area and seek refuge. Thus, we have the need for cars and the ability to get to where we need to go. Here are some survival projects that will make your car last and, hopefully, get you to your safe area with a safe ride.

Gas Siphoning

One of the key factors when you are trying to survive in certain areas of the world is how much gas you have left in your car. Additionally, if you are trying to survive an end world or lack of civilization type of situation then you are likely also trying to get to the nearest shelter or safe area that you can. Getting to that area can be quite tricky if you don't have a vehicle to get you there, which is why a lot of people attempt to keep the car for as long as it will go. In this section, we'll talk about how you can keep your car going for a very long time and how to hunt for a car that will last you the longest.

Preventing Myth-Based Crisis

Let's get a myth out of the way that you see in a ton of movies. Your vehicle cannot run on urine, no matter how bad you have to go. You need to understand the engine in order to understand why. The fuel is pumped into the cylinder chamber that goes up and down. The constant up and down motion of the cylinder creates and releases pressure. The spark plugs at the top, light the gasoline when the pressure in the cylinder chamber is at its maximum. This creates pressure in the chamber and forces the cylinder down. There's normally four cylinders and abover, which is where the term 4-Cylinder Sedan comes from. Two go up while another two go down so that there is a constant flow of rotation happening inside of the car. This, in turn, churns the generator that runs the car.

The key step in this entire process is understand that the chamber containing the cylinder is pressure and that the spark plug needs something flammable in order for the explosion to take place. Last time I checked, urine was not a flammable substance. Even the idea of poop is invalid here because albeit poop contains/ releases methane, poop, itself, is not flammable in a pressurized container. Unless you have a hybrid that has a steam-engine inside of it, you're not going to go anywhere with a water-based substance like urine.

Another myth is that you can add water to premium gas in order to get regular gas, but this simply isn't true. In fact, doing this will ruin most of the gas that you are trying to dilute because the two liquids have different densities. Having a different density usually means that they simply won't mix at all. Therefore, what can happen is that the water is used before the gas because water will usually be on the bottom of the tank. Since fuel tanks are generally gravity based, the water will be injected into the engine. Due to a lack of explosion where the liquid goes away in the form of gas, the fluid not only builds up but the fuel injectors are damage because of the different density. In other words, your current vehicles has a giant puff before it dies and needs to be repaired. You can use premium gas in cars that want regular, but you shouldn't try to dilute the gas.

Effective Siphoning

There are tons of cars out on the road and, in a world-ending situation, most cars will run their gas until the car dies. Ironically, many will not know how to remove gas from the tanks underneath the gas station cement floor. This is because the most common method of siphoning is to take a tube and suck in the gas until one can get it to the point where it will freely flow into a container for a short bit before they need to perform some more unpaid favors for the gas.

There is a better way to do this, though, and it involves a second hose. When you are siphoning gas, place a second, much shorter hose inside the same hole and cover the area in a rag. Then blow into this second hose and the pressure you cause inside of the tank will push the gas through the hose with less resistance. Obviously, you need a way to increase pressure but also prevent spillage and this is what the rag is for. The rag traps the air inside of the tank and forces the container to have more pressure, but the gas hole is another area where the gas can come out so you need a way to help stop that from occurring. The rag will catch excess and this will prevent you from wasting a lot of gas. While this method does *waste* gas, you also don't get the toxic gas in your mouth by accident.

Chapter 3 – A Portable Garden

A lot of people think of a garden as something that needs to stay in one place, but this is simply not true. You can take a garden on the road with you and even use your car as a garden. Theoretically, most gas stations will have gas for a few years before they ran out from people using them. The problem is when you have to deal with the lack of the ability to pump, which can be solved in another way that I simply won't be covering here.

The true problem of a mobile garden can be broken into two different parts. The first part is how you actually transport it and the second part is how you stabilize it. While many may think that stabilizing the plants might be the harder of this two part problem, it is actually the easier problem. All you need t do is put the garden in another container filled with water. The water will absorb the bumps of the road and gently change the axis of the bottom of the garden most of the time. Since water will always have a flat surface according to its direction with gravity, we can rely on it to stabilize the garden.

No, no. The much harder of these two issues is figuring out a way to transport it. In order to figure out how you plan to transport it, you just need to realize the crucial factors that allow a plant to grow.

- Sun

- Surface

- Wind

The first objective is to make sure that the area has enough sun for the plants to grow and this may seem obvious to most, but this has a few clever exceptions.

One would likely choose the roof to grow plants if they plan to use the car in their venture to have a portable garden, but while this may be a good spot for the sun, it is horrible if you think about the wind from the drive and the access bugs have to it from the open air above. Sure, with plants you are almost always going to have a bug problem unless you grow the plants inside, but on the roof of a car you have issues like the mosquitoes coming to nest in the pockets of water and a long list of other bugs that normally only stay in the trees rather than access plants found near the ground.

On the other hand, you also have the plants that sit inside of the window, which has the same benefit of the sun for at least half the day, but then you also get protection from the wind and the bugs because it is in an enclosed space. The only problem with this is that you don't have as much room and it can get to the point where making a portable garden becomes portable pointless.

With that said, you do have one option that can not only mean you have a portable garden, but that you can make such a garden regardless of your current circumstance. This is vitally important if you see that you might not know when you will be able to get back into a society.

Portable Garden

All you need is a plastic container, a pullable item that attaches to the back of a car, like an open trailer, a plant that you know won't kill you, and a few holes in the container. Now, just remember that a plant runs off of carbon dioxide so it will need access to the outside world, which is why I suggest putting holes inside of your container. However, these holes do not need to be big. In fact, anything smaller than a pencil hole will usually be enough to ensure that most small bugs cannot get into the container. By being able to pull this item behind you in a car or the red wagon you saw in a zombie infested house you are literally pulling your future meals on wheels.

By following standard gardening practices of rotational cropping and having a fast growing plant like a potato or some lettuce, you will have a routine amount of food. The problem then becomes scarcity. While it is great to have a garden that you can pull behind you, something like this simply won't be enough to carry you from month to month unless you want to eat potatoes and salad for the foreseeable future. This means you need to invest in something that can grow more crops, which is where you can start using shelves. On the bottom shelf, you can have something like potatoes since they don't require a lot of sun and on higher shelves, with less room, you can grow more greedy plants like the lettuces. This almost doubles the amount of food you can get, but that might, still, not be enough. Thus we need a square vertical garden.

Square Vertical Garden

Let's say you have a portable space for your garden, but it simply doesn't provide enough food for you. If we have an open trailer that we've been pulling that's of a standard size, we basically have a storage space. If you only used the floor as a means to grow plants, then you only have one layer of plants you can grow. This is not that easy to maintain, you aren't maximizing your space, and you tend to pick faster than you can grow.

With a Square Vertical Garden, you have five more layers you can grow from, maintaining them doesn't require backbending, and you will definitely grow way more than you need for one person. We need at least five wooden pallets and these will be used to hold your plants. Then you will need any type of thing that looks like a pot, a hook for each pot preferably, and a hammer with nails. You can use twice as many pallets if you have the room for it but the guidelines are simple.

Attach the first four of the pallets perpendicularly in order to create a square via the nails. All of the undersides of the pallets should be facing outward. For the top of this square, you will only nail two corners down. If you have hinges, you can easily put those on, but you can also use nails keeping in mind that you will need to replace them at some point in time. This is so that you can store necessary items in the square. Then you just put the hooks on the shelves and hook the pots on them. This should give you five areas to place plants on or ten if you were able to double it.

Chapter 4 – Personal Protection

Personal protection is vital in a survival situation and while many survivalists tend to lean towards a strong offense, having a strong defense is often *better* for humans. Humans are creatures of endurance, which is why the cheetah may run fast but we'll always win in a long haul race. Humans are the tortoises of that old fable.

Arm Shield

One of the options that you have in protecting yourself is to create a shield on your arm. Now, most would just think you could put some metal on your arm and you would be fine or you could just put some shoulder pads, but this logic is flawed.

The truth of creating a useful shield is that it is made up of three different concepts. The first concept is that you need something to hold on, which means that you need to have some type of handle. The second concept involves dealing with impact force because you may be protected from the sharp blade or the spikes on the ball, but you do not have protection from the impact force that is provided via a residual effect.

Think of it like a pan being slammed against. Sure, the thing you slam against the pan will not go through the pan but you will hear the residual sound waves that come from the impact. If you place your hand on the pan when it occurs, you will usually feel the impact and the sound waves will go inside of your hand. When a weapon hits the shield, the impact force will be much greater because the weapon is often heavier and the vibrations will usually cause an aching sensation given enough time.

Therefore, by saying all that, you need something to absorb the impact and this usually means that you need some type of rubber. You can get a rubber material with a sticky side by ordering off the internet, but so long as you have rubber you can also use a flame to heat up one side to melt it on to the protective material. Rubber will absorb the impact, but rubber isn't the only material. However, rubber is the most easily accessed material that will absorb the most amount. After all, you can find tires all over the place nowadays.

The final concept is that you need to protect your arm and this is where your choice of material is vitally important. You can choose plastic, metal, or wood. Most survivalists would only give you the option of metal or wood, but you do have the option of plastic sometimes. There are pros and cons of each.

Metal will protect you from a long list of items and will generally remain usable for a long time to come. The problem with metal is that it rusts and, when it does, the material becomes rather brittle. When it becomes brittle, you risk your shield shattering or breaking on you at, probably, the worst of times.

Wood is really great for lasting a long time because it doesn't rust and it will usually take a long time to rot. The problem with wood is that it splinters over time and a strong enough force can split the wood in half. This can make the choice of building a wooden choice lethal to what you intend to do and can result in the issue of wasted labor.

Plastic does not rot and can protect against a lot of different types of weapon. It also does not normally get hot and can be remade after it has been damaged. The problem with plastic is that the density of the plastic will determine how protective the material is. This means that if you choose to use a plastic with a relatively low density, then it may protect you against knives and pen stabs, but it won't even handle the basic bludgeon and will shatter when it has to face any real challenge.

Now that you understand all that goes into a shield, you also understand how one should be made. For myself, I normally construct a shield made out of high density plastic with rubber to absorb the blow, but I use a belt as a handle after I have nailed or screwed it into the material. Belts made out of leather are also really good at absorbing the blow before it gets to your hands, which means you can hold the shield much longer. This is important for endurance fighting. An awesome side note from our history is that we figured these principles out in medieval times, but since the warriors didn't have access to the rubber we have today they used leather instead, much like what we have in belts. This is because leather is an absorbent material and can be used as a less effective rubber.

Body Shield

The body shield isn't much different than the arm shield, but there's a small difference. Unlike the arm shield, the residual force can be much bigger and this means the shield has a much higher chance of breaking. As a result, choosing the material for the body shield can be a little different if you want the shield to be as effective as the one on your arm.

One option you can do with this is you can make a layer on top of the material you make for an arm shield to further bolster the difference of your item. This would include fiberglass cloth mixed with poly resin. You can layers these up quite high in different patterns to prevent some smaller bullets from hitting you, but nothing you make at home is going to rival what a commercially bought bullet proof riot shield can provide in terms of protection. This brings me to the warning about shields.

Warnings About Shields

Shields are meant to buy time, which is something many people who have never had to use shields don't think about. The common thought is that they are meant to provide the same cover you might get from hiding behind a car, but this is not true at all. Instead, they are designed to help you get to a safe area or to help you close the distance. They are a temporary measure and should never be seen as a permanent solution to your protective needs.

Defense Tips

While we could easily write a self-defense book, it will save you a lot of time if you just learn the core principles behind all fighting techniques. These bullets primarily explain how nearly all fighting methods work.

Watching your opponents shoulders will help you see where the attack is coming from

- Dodge outward to dodge, but dodge inward to attack

- All areas that involve joints are potential points of attack

- Do not rely on strength when you can position yourself so that gravity and motion does the work for you

- Be patient and your opponent will always give you an opening

- Do not start fights with more than one person, both verbally and while fighting.

These are the basic core principles and knowing them may be more vital than knowing any specific method of fighting. It is still good to know a form of fighting, but knowing these core principles can help out in a pinch, especially if you've never had to fight someone.

Conclusion

Welcome to the end of this book and while the book may be over, I still want to leave you with a bit of advice and a push towards the right path. In a world of survival, you need to focus on the needs instead of the wants even though the wants tend to tie in greatly with the wants. This is very important when determining what course of action you should take in order to protect yourself. An example of this is whether you should craft a boat to cross a river or use the same material to make a shield. You don't need to make a boat to cross a river unless you can't swim, but you do need to protect your body from harm or else you will die very quickly. The boat will only be used once while the shield can be used multiple times.

This is what I mean by making a choice that is based on needs versus wants. You may want to build the boat because you don't *want* to travel over the river by your lonesome, but you don't *need* to build the boat unless you can't swim. The shield could mean life or death when facing a predator though and you do *need* to protect your body from that predator.

With this in mind, when looking for survival projects and information you should evaluate your own needs before you begin to look for the material. You may find that you do not need certain projects in the long run. Alright, I suppose I have to leave you now, be safe and always watch your back for your Brutus.

FREE Bonus Reminder

If you have not grabbed it yet, please go ahead and download your special bonus report *"Preppers Survival Guide. Proven Tactics For Armed Incounters!"*

Simply Click the Button Below

OR **Go to This Page**

http://preppersliving.com/free

BONUS #2: More Free & Discounted Books & Products

Do you want to receive more Free/Discounted Books or Products?

We have a mailing list where we send out our new Books or Products when they go free or with a discount on Amazon. Click on the link below to sign up for Free & Discount Book & Product Promotions.

=> Sign Up for Free & Discount Book & Product Promotions <=

OR Go to this URL

http://zbit.ly/1WBb1Ek